I0436411

VIRTUAL

WHOLESALING SECRETS

101 (Real Estate)

How to Start

Wholesaling Real Estate with Just a Laptop,

a Phone and Internet

CLARK WALLER

COPY RIGHT

TABLE OF CONTENT

INTRODUCTION

(FROM MUD HUT TO REAL ESTATE MOGUL)

Ever ponder why certain real estate investors seem to be so successful while others struggle to make ends meet? What's the trade secret that separates the winners from the losers, the moguls from the average people?

Learn the inspirational story of Clark Waller, a self-made businessman who began his career in Vietnam living in a mud hut and eating frogs for dinner before going on to create an empire in the real estate market in the heart of America.

You will learn how Clark Waller overcame hardship, intimidation, bigotry, and countless skeptics who doubted his ability. You will also learn about how, at the age of 18, he dropped out of high school, defying all odds and driven by an unrivaled desire to succeed on his own terms.

Additionally, you will discover the strategies that Fred Schmidt used to build his fortune through real estate wholesaling—a way to make money without having to purchase, care for, or fix real estate. You will learn how to find motivated sellers, negotiate like a pro, close deals without seeing the property, and leverage the unrestricted business opportunities presented by the internet age.

You will also discover how Fred Schmidt grew his virtual wholesaling business, built a virtual crew, and automated his procedures. You will learn how he earns a living through many streams, amasses millions of social media followers, and lives the life he wants.

Not merely a biography, this book is a manual for everyone hoping to thrive in life and real estate investing. You will be pushed, inspired, and encouraged to pursue your goals with renewed vigor after reading this book.

If you're ready to learn from the best, let's grab this money!

CHAPTER 1:

HOW TO FIND MOTIVATED SELLERS ONLINE.

In the real estate industry, finding and selling properties without being the owner is referred to as *WHOLESALING.* You've already done an excellent job of defining wholesaling, outlining its benefits, and outlining the steps involved in getting started. I can help you by adding more information and examples to your overview. Here is my larger copy:

Wholesaling is a way to invest in real estate without really buying or owning the property. Finding a motivated seller who wants to sell their property quickly and reasonably is the first step, followed by finding a buyer who is willing to pay more for the property. The wholesaler acts as a middleman and profits from the difference in price between the seller and the buyer.

Wholesale is a great option for first-time real estate investors if they want to get into the business but lack resources or experience. Some reasons to consider wholesaling include the following:

Not a large sum of money is needed. Unlike other real estate investing strategies, purchasing the property, covering closing fees, and making repairs are not required while wholesaling. All that's required to finalize the deal with the seller is a little earnest money deposit. After then, for a price, the buyer may assign the contract to you. This expense could range from a few hundred to a few thousand dollars, depending on the arrangement. For example, if you find a seller who is willing to sell a $100,000 property for $60,000 and a buyer who is willing to pay $80,000, you can assign the contract to the buyer for a $20,000 fee and make $19,000 (after subtracting your deposit).

It is not necessary to obtain a license. In most areas, you can wholesale homes without a real estate license as long as you are not acting as an agent or broker for either the seller or the buyer. All you're doing is selling your contractual rights to someone else. Before wholesaling, you should, however, always review the rules and legislation in your area because other states might have stricter laws or need disclosures. Additionally, you should avoid calling the property your own while wholesaling because terms like "sell" and "buy" could imply that you are the owner. Instead, use terms like "assign" or "transfer" when referring to the contract.

You have no issues with tenants or contractors. Wholesaling is one short-term strategy that gets around holding or managing the property. You don't have to worry about collecting rent, choosing and screening tenants, or hiring professionals to fix the property. All you need to do is find a reasonable offer and an interested customer. You can save a ton of hassle, money, and time by doing this. For example, if you find a house that needs $20,000 in repairs and your monthly payments are $1,000 for the mortgage, taxes, and insurance, you will have to spend $32,000 and wait a few months to sell the house. On the other hand, selling the property wholesale and making a profit fast would save you money and headaches.

You can broaden your network and gain knowledge about the industry. Wholesaling makes it easier to learn the ins and outs of the real estate market, including how to find deals, assess homes, negotiate contracts, and finish transactions. You may also add more people to your network of contacts—buyers, sellers, agents, lenders, and other investors—who can help you grow your business and find new opportunities. For example, if you wholesale a property to a rehabber, you can become good friends with them and gain from their expertise and experience. Additionally, you can work together on future projects or they can refer you to others for deals.

IF WHOLESALERING APPEARS INTERESTING TO YOU, HERE ARE SOME ACTIONS YOU CAN TAKE TO GET STARTED:

Seek out a source of leads. You need to find motivated sellers who are willing to take a price below market for their properties. A variety of tactics are available to you, such as bandit signs, direct mail, internet ads, driving for cash, networking, and referrals. Driving around your target neighborhood and looking for homes with distressed qualities (foreclosure notices, boarded-up windows, and messy lawns) is a tactic known as "driving for dollars." You can submit an offer to buy the owners' properties if you get in contact with them.

Direct mail is the practice of sending letters or postcards to potential sellers, such as absentee owners, probate leads, or divorce leads. After that, you may follow up with calls or emails in an attempt to convince them to sell their properties. One strategy to attract sellers looking for a quick and easy transaction is to post ads online on social media platforms such as Facebook, Instagram, or Craigslist. Place posters saying "Cash for Your Home" or "We Buy Houses" on busy intersections or streets, and sellers will contact you with an offer that interests them. This is referred to as the "bandit sign" tactic.

Referrals are a way to obtain leads since someone you know—friends, family, or coworkers—may know someone who is trying to sell their house. Meeting other real estate professionals—such as agents, lenders, or investors—through events or group memberships in online forums, real estate clubs, or seminars is known as networking. You can get recommendations or leads from them.

Evaluate the property and the contract. You need to perform market and property research in order to determine the after repair value (ARV) and the cost of repairs. The ARV is the estimated market worth of the property following repairs and sale preparation. You can utilize online tools such as Zillow, Trulia, or Red fin, or contact a local real estate agent, to find similar houses that have sold lately in the same area and with similar features. The repair charges cover the anticipated expenses of fixing the property and making it marketable again. Online calculators such as HomeAdvisor can be used to estimate the cost of repairs such as flooring, painting, plumbing, electrical, or roofing. You can also ask contractors for quotes.

It's also necessary to figure out the maximum allowable offer (MAO) you can make to the seller and the minimum acceptable profit (MAP) you can make from the deal. The MAO is the highest price you can spend for the property and still make a profit. One could use the formula below: Repair costs = ARV x 0.7 = MAO. The 0.7 factor explains why wholesalers usually aim for a 30% discount when buying properties. The minimum acceptable profit (MAP) is the amount of profit you are willing to accept from the deal. You can also set your own criteria, like a percentage of the ARV, a monetary amount, or a return on investment (ROI). Your MAP, for example, would look like this: If you have a $1,000 deposit and your objective is to make at least 10% ROI on your deals, then MAP = Deposit x (1 + ROI) = $1,000 x (1 + 0.1) = $1,100.

Don't Be Silent And Sign The Contract.
You have to contact the vendor and make them an offer that satisfies their requirements as well as your profit margin. It's also a good idea to include a clause that lets you assign the contract to another buyer or back out if no bidder is found. A standard purchase agreement or a unique wholesaling contract might specify the terms and circumstances of the sale, including the price, the closing date, the earnest money deposit, the inspection period, and the contingencies. You may also utilize an assignment agreement or purchase agreement addendum that states that you may assign the contract to another buyer for a premium and that the seller agrees to this arrangement. You should always have a lawyer review any contracts before you sign them to make sure you are in compliance with all state laws and regulations.

Find a buyer, then transfer the contract to them. Promoting the property and the agreement to potential buyers, such as cash buyers, rehabbers, wholesalers, and landlords, is essential. Using a range of strategies, such as flyers, email lists, web platforms, and word-of-mouth marketing, you may promote the property and the deal and attract buyers who are looking for a good opportunity. You should include relevant information in your marketing brochures, such as the address, photos, ARV, cost of repairs, asking price, and assignment fee. You must additionally examine the buyers to make sure they have the means and ability to finish the deal. You can ask for documentation of their finances, such as bank statements, credit letters, or pre-approval letters from lenders, to verify their financial capability.

You can also ask for references, such as past business transactions or client endorsements, to confirm their legality and reputation. Once a buyer has been identified, you need to provide them the contract in return for cash, then collect your profit at closing. You may use an assignment agreement or an addendum to the purchase agreement to transfer your rights and obligations under the contract to the buyer and to get payment for this service. You should also notify the seller and the title company about the assignment and provide them with the necessary documentation, such as the assignment agreement, the evidence of funds, and the earnest money deposit. You should also be present at the closing or send a representative on your behalf to make sure everything goes according to plan and that you are paid.

Wholesaling real estate is a simple and easy way to make money, but it also requires skill, diligence, and commitment.

CHAPTER 2:

HOW TO FIND MOTIVATED SELLERS ONLINE

Real estate investors need to be able to find motivated sellers online in order to find great bargains and grow their business. Motivated sellers are real estate owners who are prepared to sell their homes due to a range of circumstances, such as downsizing, financial difficulties, divorce, inheritance, or relocation. They are willing to sell their properties for less money or under better terms, which benefits both the buyer and the seller.

While there are many techniques to search the internet for motivated sellers, the following are some of the most effective ones to attempt:

Utilize online services that are devoted to connecting motivated investors and sellers.

With the help of these tools, you may view and assess millions of US properties and filter them based on attributes like equity, vacancy, foreclosure, liens, or owner details. These platforms also enable you to follow up on leads and deals and communicate directly with vendors via email, direct mail, or phone. For example, a reliable source can be utilized to find buildings with a high equity and low occupancy rate. Then, by sending the owner a customized letter or postcard, you can make an offer to purchase the property for cash. Deal Machine can also be used to recognize distressed signs on buildings, such as overgrown lawns or boarded-up windows, and then send them an email or text message expressing interest in helping to resolve the situation. Real e flow can also be used to find homes that have tax liens on them or that are in pre-foreclosure. Once you've found a property, you can contact the owner or pay them a visit to try to arrange a bargain.

Search for motivating terms on popular real estate websites such as Realtor.com, Zillow, Red fin, or Trulia. The following terms can be used: "must sell," "as-is," "fixer upper," "cash only," "motivated seller," "price reduced," or "owner financing." You should also look for properties that have had multiple price drops or have been on the market for a long time, as these may be signs of a motivated seller. For example, you can look through Zillow's listings for properties that have the term "must sell" in the listing description and sort them by lowest price or longest time for sale.

You may also use Trulia to look for homes with the phrase "motivated seller" in the title. You can also narrow down your search by price per square foot or the amount of price adjustments. Another tool you may use to find homes with the status "price reduced" is Realtor.com. You can compare the homes with the original listing price or the median listing price in the area. Red fin can also be used to find properties with the "as-is" characteristics and assess the cost and state of repair.

To attract motivated sellers, use targeted adverts on social media platforms such as Facebook, Instagram, and YouTube to promote your website or landing page. Advertisements such as "We buy houses fast for cash," "Sell your house in 7 days," or "No fees, no commissions, no repairs" are instances of how you might provide the seller a resolution. You can also use case studies, images that show before and after, or testimonial films to show off your skills and results. Ads can be tailored to specific audiences according to their location, interests, habits, or demographics in order to maximize cost-effectiveness and conversions.

You could, for example, utilize Facebook to create a video ad highlighting a happy seller who sold you their house in only one week, and then target people who live in your neighborhood, are over forty, and have recently changed their marital status with that advertisement. You can use an Instagram photo ad that contrasts the before and after of a house you bought and fixed to target people who live in your neighborhood, are interested in home improvement, and have recently browsed for real estate agents. You can also create a video advertisement on YouTube that explains how you can help sellers avoid foreclosure. You can use this advertisement to target people who live in your neighborhood, have visited websites about preventing foreclosures, and have watched real estate investing videos.

Create a blog or podcast that provides intelligent content to motivated sellers, and employ SEO techniques to raise its search engine ranking. Talks or writings on topics like "How to sell a house with liens," "How to sell an inherited house," "How to avoid foreclosure," or "How to sell a house during a divorce" are examples of topics that speak to the sellers' worries. You can also use keywords, backlinks, meta tags, and other SEO strategies to improve your visibility and authority on Google and other search engines. Tools are also useful for tracking performance, researching keywords, and analyzing competitors. For example, use SEMrush to find the most popular and relevant keywords for your niche. You can then use those keywords in your podcast episodes or blog posts. Ah references can also be utilized to find the most important and respectable websites in your field. After that, you can try to get backlinks from these websites by commenting, guest blogging, or sharing. With the help of these tools, you can monitor your traffic, ranking, and conversion rates and make any necessary adjustments to your content.

Engage in online networks and forums where motivated sellers gather, and respond to their questions or concerns with helpful answers, hints, or advice. You can also share your own stories, successes, or experiences with the suppliers to build rapport and confidence. By adding a link to your website or landing page in your signature or profile, you can also invite sellers to contact you for more information or a free consultation. You can also answer questions and provide recommendations to sellers who are struggling or in need of direction. You may stay up to date on topics like foreclosure, real estate investing, and house sales, and you can provide extensive and informative answers to perplexed or curious sellers.

These are some of the best ways to find motivated sellers on the internet, while there are other options as well. You can also employ email marketing, webinars, online events, and recommendations to generate more leads and revenues. The key is to experiment and modify your methods until you find the ones that are most effective for you and your target audience. Additionally, you ought to be creative, reliable, and client-focused. It might be challenging to find motivated sellers online, but it can also be incredibly helpful for growing your real estate investing business by giving you more chances to close deals. I hope this makes it clearer how to find motivated suppliers online and why it's a good idea to do so.

CHAPTER 3:

HOW TO USE SKIP TRACING TO LOCATE AND CONTACT LEADS

Finding and getting in touch with people who are difficult to get in touch with or who have bypassed their usual lines of contact is known as "skip tracking." In the real estate sector, skip tracing can be used to locate and connect with motivated sellers, absentee owners, or distressed homeowners who might be willing to sell at a discount or under favorable conditions.

Here are some guidelines for locating and contacting real estate leads via skip tracing:

Establish your target market and criterion. You have to know who you are looking for and what kind of properties they have. For example, you could target homeowners who are in arrears on their mortgage, are going through a divorce, or have tax liens against them. These signify a need to sell quickly or financial trouble. Online systems make it possible to access and evaluate millions of properties across the United States by allowing you to filter properties based on various characteristics such as equity, vacancy, foreclosure, liens, or owner information. These websites can also provide you with helpful information, such as area demographics, property values, and market trends, to help you narrow down your search and identify the best opportunities.

Find the leads' contact information. You need to find the leads' phone numbers, email addresses, or mailing addresses in order to contact them and make an offer. can be used to match and append the contact details of the leads to their properties online. Not only can these solutions provide you with additional features like marketing campaigns, CRM integration, and skip tracking automation, but they can also help you verify the accuracy and timeliness of the data. One can use search engines, social media, public data, and credit reports to find additional or alternative means of contacting the leads. You should be careful to follow any privacy or anti-spam regulations when using these sources.

Talk to the leads and build a relationship. You must establish contact with the leads and earn their confidence. You can get in touch with the leads via phone, text, email, direct mail, or face-to-face meetings in order to address their problem and establish a relationship. You should also follow up with the leads until you hear back, whether it's positive or negative. You can use scripts, templates, or examples to help you build your messages and responses. Avoid being coercive, antagonistic, or deceitful; instead, strive to be kind, understanding, and professional. You must also try to understand the leads in order to tailor your offer to their needs, goals, and pain areas. You should also be prepared to address questions, denials, and objections and refute them with supporting data, advice, and benefits.

Make a deal and close the deal. Once the terms and price of the deal have been negotiated, you need the leads to sign a contract. You should also evaluate the property and figure out the maximum allowed offer (MAO) and minimum acceptable profit (MAP). The MAO is the most amount you can spend on a property and still make a profit, and the MAP is the lowest profit you are ready to accept on a deal. It is also advisable that you use a standard purchase agreement or a specific wholesaling contract, and include a clause allowing you to assign the contract to another buyer or to terminate it if no buyer is identified. Before you sign any contracts, you should have them reviewed by a lawyer, and you should follow all state laws and regulations.

Finding and contacting real estate leads with the use of skip tracing is a successful strategy that can result in more sales and financial gain. However, it also requires knowledge, diligence, and commitment, as well as legal and moral execution. I hope this makes it clearer how to use skip tracing to locate and contact real estate leads. Kindly don't hesitate to ask me any queries.

CHAPTER 4:

HOW TO DISCUSE LIKE A KING OVER THE PHONE

Every real estate agent need to know how to negotiate, whether they are buying or selling a property. However, since you have to persuade the other party with your words, tone, and voice, it could be challenging to bargain over the phone. Here are some tips for conducting a professional real estate phone negotiation, along with some scenarios in which you can apply them:

Prepare yourself before the call. Before you answer the phone, be sure you've finished your homework and have all the information you need. Recognize your options, your financial situation, and your goals. Look into the market, the property, and the other party. Consider their requirements, wants, and objections when you prepare your counteroffers and responses in advance. Establish a clear plan and script for the discussion, but be flexible and prepared to modify it as required.

For example, if you are a wholesaler looking to buy a house from a motivated seller, you need know the following before the conversation:

The property's after-repair value and fair market value; the anticipated costs of holding and repairs; the highest amount that can be offered and the least amount that can be profited from the deal; the seller's name, contact information, and circumstances; the common objections and questions that sellers may have and how to respond to them

1. Key characteristics and value propositions of your offer, along with presentation tips

2. The phases and timetable of the closure procedure, together with their descriptions

You should also write a script outlining the main points and questions you want to cover during the call, such as:

• Gratitude and synopsis

• The purpose and timetable of the call; • Orientation and qualification questions; • Property and situation assessment questions

• Outline the value of the offer.

• Handling objections and closing thoughts

• The aftermath and future actions

However, you should also be prepared to deviate from the plan if the conversation takes a different turn and to adjust your offer and strategy in response to the seller's questions and remarks.

Establish rapport and confidence The first few minutes of the call are crucial for establishing a friendly yet professional relationship with the other party. Greetings and introductions should be given, along with the reason for your call. Make frequent use of their name, show interest in and respect for their situation and point of view. Avoid digressions and disagreements by paying close attention and showing empathy when you listen. Use open-ended questions to elicit information and feedback while mirroring their language and tone in order to establish rapport and trust.

For example, if you're a wholesaler calling a motivated seller, you could start the conversation like this:

Who's that, John? This is Mike from ABC Solutions. "How are you feeling today?"

"I observed your property at 123 Main Street and I'm calling to express my interest in buying it."Would you like to discuss it for a little while?"

"Very good; many thanks. I appreciate your time. So tell me, what made you decide to sell your house."

"I see, that's terrible to hear. That must be challenging. For what duration have you been the land's owner?"

That's a long time, wow. You must have a great deal of recollections. Which aspects of the property catch your attention the most?

See how the caller uses the seller's name, shows empathy and curiosity, and asks open-ended questions to build rapport and trust. The caller also imitates the seller's tempo and loudness, using slang terms like "wow" and "tough" to match the seller's vocabulary and tone.

Consider the advantages and worth. When making an offer or proposal, give the other party's benefits and value more weight than the conditions or cost. Explain how your offer will meet their needs, satisfy their wants, or resolve their issue. In order to bolster your claims and establish your authority, offer statistics, evidence, and reports. In your pitch, highlight the unique features and advantages of your offer and draw favorable comparisons with comparable goods and services offered by competitors.

For example, if you are a wholesaler and you would like to purchase a property from a motivated seller, you could offer the following:

I can make you a cash offer of $100,000 for your property, with a closing date of as soon as seven days, based on the information you provided and the state of the market.

I realize that this might not be the best deal out there, but let me explain why I think this is a great chance for you. First off, there are no commissions, fees, closing costs, or repairs to worry about. I'll buy your property as-is and take care of all the costs. Put another way, you can avoid problems and inconveniences and end up saving thousands of dollars.

Second, you won't have to wait months to sell your home or deal with any contingencies, inspections, appraisals, or financing issues. Given that I have the funds on hand, I can close as soon as you like or even in as little as seven days. This suggests that you can sell your possessions and move on with your life quite soon.

Thirdly, there are no listings, negotiations, or showings to deal with. I will do my best to make things as simple and uncomplicated as possible for you. You only need to sign the contract; I'll take care of the rest. Even the closing location and time are customizable to suit your needs.

I have helped hundreds of sellers in similar situations, and every single one of them was happy with the way things turned out. Here are some testimonials from satisfied clients who can vouch for my integrity and expertise.

Pay attention to how the caller stresses the benefits and value of the offer over its conditions or price. The caller explains how the offer will meet the seller's requirements, satisfy their desires, and resolve their issue. The caller often offers data, statistics, and testimony to back up their claims and demonstrate their reliability. Additionally, the caller highlights the unique features and advantages of the offer and presents it in a positive light in comparison to competitors or other possibilities.

Make deliberate use of pauses and quiet. Pausing and remaining silent during phone conversations can be useful tactics because they can make the other person feel nervous, suspenseful, or curious, which can influence how they behave. Pauses and silences can be employed to highlight a point, exude assurance or authority, evoke a response or an emotion, or buy yourself some time to gather your thoughts. However, employ silence and pauses with care as they might backfire and lead to miscommunication, boredom, or even hostility.

To create a sense of urgency and scarcity, for example, if you are a wholesaler putting in a bid to buy real estate from a motivated seller, you can employ pauses and silences like these:

John, I have to let you know that this is a very short-lived offer. I have other properties I'm thinking about buying, but I can only buy one more this month. So, if you want to take advantage of this opportunity, you must act fast. If not, I may need to look for a better deal. (Give it a moment.)"

"John, how are you feeling? Are you prepared to accept my offer and complete this transaction now? (Hold off on speaking until the vendor responds.)

Remember that the caller employs calm and pauses to wait for a response from the seller, emphasizes urgency and scarcity, and conveys confidence and authority. Tension and suspense are also increased since the caller influences the seller's thoughts and behavior.

Complete the transaction. If you and the other party have reached a compromise or an understanding, don't hesitate to close the deal. Make sure they comprehend and accept the agreement by going over its essential terms and conditions. Tell them how much you appreciate and are satisfied, and ask for their signature and commitment. After the transaction is finished, provide a formal confirmation and a statement of appreciation, and maintain communication during that period.

For example, if you are a wholesaler and you have worked out a deal with a motivated seller, you could sign the agreement like this: "Great, John, I'm glad we were able to come to an agreement. Allow me to quickly go over the terms and key components of the agreement to make sure we are both on the same page. I'm willing to pay $100,000 in cash for your property, plus I'll take care of all the upkeep, fees, commissions, and closing costs. I'll buy your house as is, and I can close as soon as you want or even as soon as seven days from now. Listings, showings, and negotiations are not involved. You only need to sign the contract; I'll take care of the rest. Does that sound accurate?

Fantastic, John I'm happy that you're satisfied. Here, we both stand to gain from one another. All we need right now is your signature and commitment. Depending on your preference, I can send you the contract by email, fax, or postal once it's ready. How would you prefer to receive it?"

"All good, John. I will send you the contract by email right now. Please review it carefully and sign it at once. Once I obtain the signed contract, I will start the closing process and keep you updated on my progress. Do you have any questions or concerns before we end the call?

Not at all? Wonderful, John. Thank you for your cooperation and belief. I appreciate your company and am forward to collaborate with you. I'll respond to you right away. I'm hoping you have a fantastic day. Goodbye."

Observe how the caller wraps off the deal by restating the conditions and key details and getting the seller to sign off on their understanding and acceptance. The caller calls to thank and express satisfaction, and asks for the seller's word and signature. Together with sending a formal confirmation and thank-you card, the caller follows up till the agreement is fulfilled.

To bargain like a king over the phone in real estate requires preparation, communication, and persuasive abilities in addition to a positive and professional mindset. By following these tips, you may achieve your real estate goals and improve the efficiency and outcomes of your phone conversations.

CHAPTER 5:

HOW TO USE VIRTUAL TOOLS TO CLOSE DEALS WITHOUT HAVING TO SEE THE PROPERTY

Both buyers and sellers usually have to act quickly to secure the best offers in the competitive and fast-paced real estate market. However, there are times when viewing a property in person before making an offer or completing a deal is not feasible or practical. This is especially important for remote investors, who may be thinking about properties dispersed throughout multiple cities, states, or even countries.

Thanks to technology improvements, real estate transactions can now be conducted online without a physical inspection of the property. With the help of many virtual tools, you may evaluate, market, negotiate, and close agreements online and save a lot of time, money, and hassle. We'll examine some of the most popular and practical online resources in this post so you can complete real estate transactions even if you are unable to see the property in person.

VR Tours and 3D Models

One of the most important aspects of buying or selling a home is getting a feel for its layout, features, condition, and mood. Having said that, it can be challenging to do this without actually seeing the property. This explains why virtual tours and 3D models are such useful tools in real estate transactions.

Interactive images or videos that allow you to visually explore a location are called virtual tours. Being able to move about, zoom in, and view things from various angles gives you a realistic and immersive experience. For additional information or guidance, some virtual tours also come with audio or narration.

3D models are digital representations of a property that you can view and interact with on a computer or mobile device. It is possible to rotate, enlarge, measure, and change the property's colors, furnishings, and lighting. With the use of 3D models, you can assess a property's potential and pinpoint any issues or flaws.

You can use virtual tours and 3D models to show prospective buyers your house and examine a property you are interested in purchasing. They can also save you time and money because you won't have to travel to the property or hire a professional photographer or filmmaker.

Neighborhood Reviews and Ratings on the Internet

The neighborhood and location of a house greatly affect its value and desirability. However, it may be hard to acquire a sense of the neighborhood without visiting it. For this reason, real estate transactions can benefit greatly from online neighborhood reviews and ratings.

Online neighborhood ratings and reviews are websites and apps that provide you insights and advice on a variety of local issues, such as schools, safety, facilities, demography, and culture. You can also see maps, photos, and videos of the neighborhood and compare it to other neighborhoods in the area.

Online neighborhood evaluations and ratings can help you find the best areas for your needs and preferences, in addition to marketing your house to potential buyers looking for a specific kind of location.

Tools for Interaction and Communication Online

Two of the most crucial aspects of completing a real estate deal are teamwork and communication. You will have to arrange and communicate with the buyer, seller, agent, lender, appraiser, inspector, title company, and lawyer, among other parties, in order to close the sale. Doing this without really meeting them can be difficult and time-consuming. For real estate transactions, online collaboration and communication tools are therefore essential.

Programs or software that enable you to communicate and collaborate with others online using text, voice, video, email, chat, and other channels are known as tools for online communication and collaboration. You may exchange files, contracts, documents, and signatures in addition to setting up meetings, appointments, and reminders.

By utilizing internet resources for collaboration and communication, you may reduce errors, hold-ups, and miscommunication. You can streamline and expedite these procedures with the use of these technologies. You can also save time and money because you won't need to print and ship documents or fly to meet with the other parties.

Web-Based Resources for Calculations and Analysis of Real Estate

Among the most difficult tasks to complete during a real estate transaction are analysis and computation. A property's market value, rental income, cash flow, return on investment, and closing costs are just a few of the many numbers and data that must be computed and reviewed. It could be challenging and time-consuming to finish if you don't have a tool or a specialist to help you. For this reason, online tools for real estate computation and analysis are quite helpful in real estate transactions.

Online real estate analysis and calculation tools are websites or apps that help you use a range of data and formulas to analyze and calculate various aspects of a real estate transaction. You can also change the settings and assumptions, and generate reports and visualizations.

You may use online real estate analysis and calculation tools, make informed decisions, and negotiate and close agreements more quickly and easily. You can save money and time because you don't need to hire an expert or use a spreadsheet.

Last Words

Closing real estate transactions remotely is now convenient and possible thanks to modern virtual solutions. With the aid of these technologies, you may evaluate, market, negotiate, and close deals online and potentially save time, money, and hassle. However, you should also proceed with caution and diligence, as buying or selling real estate has some risks and challenges that are unavoidable. Always use due diligence, verify the information's accuracy, and, if required, consult an expert. To closing your virtual trade, cheers!

CHAPTER 6:

HOW TO BUILD A FORMIDABLE VIRTUAL WHOLESALING TEAM

Wholesaling is a popular and profitable strategy for real estate investors who want to find and flip transactions quickly and easily. However, wholesaling may also be challenging and time-consuming, especially if you try to do everything by yourself.

For this reason, a lot of prosperous wholesalers choose to assemble a group of experts who can assist them in different areas of their company, including lead generation, contract negotiations, marketing, transaction analysis, closure, and more.

But what if you wanted to wholesale properties somewhere other than your local neighborhood? How do you manage a team that is spread across several locations and time zones?

In this case, virtual wholesaling can be useful. The activity of selling real estate remotely while working and corresponding with your group, purchasers, and sellers through internet tools and platforms is known as virtual wholesaling.

By assembling a virtual wholesaling team, you may capitalize on people's skills and experience, expand your business faster, and get access to more chances and financial benefit in any market you choose.

But how could one form a virtual wholesaling team? Which protocols and best practices ought I to follow? Here are some guidelines to help you get started.

Determine your goals and aspirations.

Before you start hiring and onboarding virtual team members, you need to have a clear idea of the objectives and operations of your company.

What are your immediate and long-term goals? What monthly deal volume do you hope to achieve? Which markets do you intend to concentrate on? What is the budget, and what is the expected return? What are your core beliefs and mission statement?

Having a clear vision and direction for your business can help you attract and retain the best employees who will help you reach your objectives.

CHOOSE WHICH JOB AND POSITIONS YOU MUST ASSIGN TO OTHER PEOPLE.

The next step is to determine what obligations and tasks you need to delegate to your virtual team. This will depend on a number of factors, including your preferences, financial status, skills, and shortcomings.

The following are typical roles and responsibilities that wholesalers contract out:

Lead generation and marketing: You should set up and maintain your website, social media accounts, direct mail, online ads, search engine optimization, and other marketing channels in order to generate leads from motivated sellers.

Lead qualification and subsequent action: This means sorting and qualifying incoming leads, verifying the information is correct, and following up with the leads until they are ready to be sold.

Researching the market and the property, comparing prices, calculating the ARV and MAO, and making an offer to the sellers are all part of the process of analyzing the deal and making an offer.

This stage of the procedure consists of deal closing, contract preparation and delivery, documentation management, and communication with the title company.

Buyer relations and decision-making: This involves deciding on an assignment fee, promoting and soliciting agreements to a list of cash purchasers, and concluding contracts.

You may choose to outsource some or all of these tasks based on your degree of expertise, availability, and financial limitations. It is also feasible to contract out non-wholesale-related services like as bookkeeping, accounting, legal, and administrative work.

SELECT AND USE THE TOP APPLICANTS

Once you've decided the positions and tasks you need to delegate, you can start looking for the best people to join your virtual team.

There are several ways to locate and recruit virtual team members, such as:

asking your network's wholesalers, other investors, or industry experts for recommendations.

posting job advertisements on websites.

use social media sites to find possible employees.

Using a virtual assistant agency or company that can provide you with skilled and pre-screened virtual assistants.

You should look for the following qualities in a virtual team member:

Experience and skills relevant to the role and the tasks you need them to perform.

Good interpersonal and collaborative skills, especially in written and spoken English

dependable and trustworthy, with a track record of finishing excellent job on time and under budget.

Adaptable and versatile, capable of working with a variety of tools and systems across multiple time zones.

motivated and enthusiastic, with a positive mindset and a desire to grow and learn.

To ensure that candidates are qualified and suitable for the role, it is a good idea to conduct interviews, background checks, and reference checks.

IMPROVE AND INCLUDE YOUR REMOTE WORKFORCE

For your virtual team members to perform their jobs efficiently and promptly after hiring, they must receive the appropriate training and onboarding.

You should take the following steps to set up and orient your remote team:

Provide them with a thorough job description that outlines all of their expectations, goals, and obligations.

Give them access to your calendar, phone, email, and CRM, as well as any other tools and systems they need to finish their work.

Provide them with training materials, including as checklists, templates, scripts, videos, and manuals, that explain how to perform their duties and follow corporate policies and procedures.

Provide them with coaching, assistance, and feedback to help them improve their skills and performance, particularly in the beginning.

To motivate them and express your gratitude for their work, provide them incentives such as commissions, bonuses, testimonials, or shout-outs.

WORK WITH YOUR REMOTE TEAM TO INTEGRATE AND COORDINATES

The next step is to regularly monitor and communicate with your remote workforce to make sure they are adhering to your goals and strategies.

Some suggested strategies for managing and communicating with your remote staff are as follows:

Set acceptable and fair objectives and deadlines for each task and project, and monitor its progress and results.

Communicate with them frequently and consistently over a range of channels, including as chat, phone, text, video, and email, to keep them informed and up to date.

Call regular meetings to discuss the successes, challenges, and overall status of the team. Examples of these meetings may be daily team meetings, weekly reviews, or monthly reports.

Assign duties and responsibilities and share documents, files, and information using Dropbox, Trello, and Google Drive to foster collaboration and teamwork.

By using platforms to facilitate in-person encounters with your team members and exhibiting interest in and concern for each person as an individual, you can build rapport and trust.

Last Words

By harnessing the strength of others, scaling your operations, and gaining access to more deals and earnings in whatever market you choose, building a virtual wholesale team can help you grow your real estate business.

Creating a virtual wholesale team also involves effective planning, hiring, training, managing, and communication to ensure that your team is productive, efficient, and aligned with your vision and goals.

By following the suggestions and guidelines in this article, you can establish a virtual wholesaling team to assist in the growth of your real estate business and the achievement of your wholesaling objectives.

CHAPTER 7:

HOW TO PROSPER IN YOUR VIRTUAL WHOLESALING BUSINESS

Virtual wholesaling makes it feasible to find and flip properties in any market without having to personally inspect them. Nonetheless, if you like to expand your virtual wholesaling business, you will need to possess exceptional scaling abilities.

You must simultaneously increase your volume, income, and profit in order to scale your virtual wholesaling firm while maintaining or improving your efficiency, quality, and customer satisfaction. Scaling also means expanding your prospects, network, and reach by venturing into new areas and niches.

But how can you expand your wholesale online business? Which strategies and techniques should be applied? These tips will help you build and develop your online wholesale real estate business.

1. *Automate and systematize your processes.*

Systematization and automation are crucial for expanding your virtual wholesaling business. Automation and systematization refer to the use of tools, software, and systems to streamline and accelerate business processes, including lead generation, marketing, transaction analysis, contract administration, closing, and disposition.

Process systematization and automation can help you save time, money, and energy. Additionally, you can reduce tension, mistakes, and delays. In addition, you can track and evaluate your performance and outcomes, as well as increase your productivity, consistency, and scalability.

Some tools and software that can help you automate and standardize your practices are as follows:

[Batch Leads]: A powerful tool that lets you find, connect with, and close more sales. Features include email marketing, SMS marketing, ring-less voicemail, list stacking, skip tracing, and more.

[REI kit]: A comprehensive platform with tools for evaluating and analyzing any kind of real estate, such as comparables, an ARV calculator, a rehab estimate, and a deal analyzer.

[Docu Sign]: A well-known platform that helps you manage and sign contracts online with features like e-signature, document generation, workflow automation, and more.

2. AWARD AND CONTRACT YOUR WORK

Another key to expanding your virtual wholesaling business is to outsource and delegate your labor. Outsourcing and delegating is the process of selecting and training people to help you with tasks like marketing, lead qualification, transaction analysis, contract negotiation, closure, and disposition.

By outsourcing and delegating your job, you may benefit from the expertise of others, save up time, and focus on your main goals. You could increase your capacity, quality, and profitability by diversifying your network and staff.

Here are some tips for delegating and contracting out your work:

Employing virtual helpers: Remote workers known as virtual assistants (VAs) can help you with a variety of technical, administrative, or creative tasks, such as managing emails, conducting research, managing social media, and more. On-site virtual assistant hiring is offered.

Employing telemarketers: Cold callers, who work remotely, can help you contact and qualify prospects by using phone calls, scripts, and CRM systems. - Employing managers of acquisitions: Acquisition managers are either local or remote staff members who may help you with the analysis and negotiation of your purchases through the use of tools, software, and contracts. On-site hiring is possible for acquisition managers. Managers of hiring disposition: Disposition managers, who may be on-site or remote staff, can help you sell and promote your contracts by providing resources, buyer lists, and tools. Marketplaces provide positions as disposition managers.

3. ESTABLISH LINKS AND WORK WITH OTHER DISTRIBUTORS

The third crucial element for expanding your virtual wholesaling business is networking and building partnerships with other wholesalers. Other wholesalers can help you find and flip more sales by trading leads, contracts, buyers, and resources. This is the nature of partnerships and networking.

Working together and networking with other wholesalers can help you increase your exposure, opportunities, and reach. Additionally, you can learn from their strategies, perceptions, and experiences. Additionally, you may build situations where everyone wins and increase recommendations, trust, and reputation.

The following are some methods for networking and cooperating with other wholesalers:

registering for online forums and groups: Through these online forums, you can interact and exchange messages with other wholesalers who are involved in your target markets or niches by sending questions, comments, and criticism. Online forums and groups are accessible through platforms.

Taking part in online events and webinars: These events allow you an opportunity to network with and learn from other wholesalers who are leaders or influencers in your industry by having speeches, Q&A sessions, and interviews. You can take part in online events and webinars that are held by websites.

Even though expanding your virtual wholesaling business is challenging, it is possible and profitable if you follow the right steps and use the right strategies. By systematizing and automating your operations, outsourcing and delegating your tasks, networking, and establishing alliances with other wholesalers, you may grow and scale your virtual real estate wholesaling firm and achieve your desired results and goals.

CONCLUSION:

THE SECRETS OF WHOLESALING AND THE INFLUENCE OF MENTALITY

Wholesaling is a fantastic strategy for real estate investors who want to find and close deals quickly and easily without assuming personal debt, credit, or risk. You can make money wholesaling by facilitating transactions between motivated vendors and cash buyers and collecting a fee.

However, wholesaling is not a simple or quick approach to make a lot of money. Wholesaling requires persistence, diligence, and commitment in addition to the required procedures, knowledge, and skills. Wholesaling also requires a strong mentality that will help you get past the challenges, obstacles, and fears you will inevitably face on your journey.

In this post, we've discussed some of the key components of wholesaling, such as:

The benefits of wholesaling, such as its low entry barrier, flexibility, and enormous profit potential. Through wholesaling, you can gain knowledge of the ins and outs of real estate investing, broaden your network, and generate cash flow without having to cope with the hassles of property ownership or management.

the processes and activities associated with wholesaling, including as transaction analysis, offer creation, contract signing, and contract selling, as well as lead generation. The first steps in wholesaling are to find motivated sellers who are willing to sell their properties at a discount and then to find cash buyers who are looking for reasonable deals. After that, the buyer can claim the contract for a price.

Websites, applications, software, and platforms are among the tools and resources that might help you with whole selling. Wholesaling can be made easier and more efficient by utilizing technology to automate and simplify your business. Examples of this technology include CRM systems, lead generation tools, deal analysis software, contract templates, and online markets.

The tips and techniques that will help you succeed in wholesaling, including networking, marketing, outsourcing, and scaling. You may improve and extend your wholesaling firm by employing tried-and-true strategies like creating a strong marketing plan, building rapport with customers and sellers, delegating tasks to team members or virtual assistants, and broadening your portfolio.

We have also discussed some of the key components of attitude, such as:

The importance of your mentality, which encompasses your attitudes, habits, and beliefs, and how these affect your success as a wholesaler. Wholesaling may be impacted by your mindset, which includes how you see yourself, your abilities, your opportunities, your challenges, and how you handle them. Positivity and empowerment give you more power than a pessimistic and limiting outlook.

The various mentalities and mindset kinds, such as fixed vs progressive, victim versus victor, and scarcity versus abundance Wholesaling can be approached and practiced with a variety of mindsets, such as: victim mindset, which places blame on other people and external factors for your failures; growth mindset, which holds that you can develop and learn via work and feedback; scarcity mindset, which emphasizes lack and competition; abundance mindset, which emphasizes possibilities and teamwork; and victor mindset, which accepts responsibility and takes action for your success.

techniques and strategies that can help you shift your perspective, such as affirmations, gratitude, meditation, and visualization. Wholesaling can be enhanced and supported by using mental skills like thankfulness, which acknowledges and appreciates what you have accomplished, meditation, which calms and clears your mind and emotions, and visualization, which creates realistic, clear visions of your intended objectives.

It is our genuine hope that this article has provided you with the motivation and inspiration to start or grow your wholesaling business and to develop a positive mindset that will help you achieve your goals.

Remember that even if wholesaling is a magical strategy, magic does not exist. It's a skill that can be learned and developed with the right mindset, knowledge, and work.

Why are you hesitant, then? Start your adventure now to benefit from the beauty of wholesaling and the power of thinking in real estate.